Funding Provided by
Supervisor Mark DeSaulnier
District IV
Contra Costa County
Board of Supervisors

SPORTS HEROES AND LEGENDS™

David Beckham

Read all of the books in this exciting, action-packed biography series!

Hank Aaron

Muhammad Ali

Lance Armstrong

David Beckham

Barry Bonds

Roberto Clemente

Sasha Cohen

Joe DiMaggio

Tim Duncan

Dale Earnhardt Jr.

Doug Flutie

Lou Gehrig

Wayne Gretzky

Derek Jeter

Sandy Koufax

Michelle Kwan

Mickey Mantle

Jesse Owens

Alex Rodriguez

Wilma Rudolph

Annika Sorenstam

Ichiro Suzuki

Jim Thorpe

Tiger Woods

SPORTS HEROES AND LEGENDS™

David Beckham

by Ken Pendleton

Twenty 3 1901 04269 0455 /Minneapolis

Twenty-First Century Books
A division of Lerner Publishing Group, Inc.
241 First Avenue North
Minneapolis, MN 55401 U.S.A.

Website address: www.lernerbooks.com

Cover photograph:
© Eddie Keogh/Reuters/CORBIS

Library of Congress Cataloging-in-Publication Data

Pendleton, Ken.
    David Beckham / by Ken Pendleton.
        p.   cm. — (Sports heroes and legends)
    Includes bibliographical references and index.
    ISBN 978–0–8225–7161–2 (lib. bdg. : alk. paper)
    1. Beckham, David, 1975-—Juvenile literature. 2. Soccer players—England—Biography—Juvenile literature. I. Title.
    GV942.7.B43P46 2007
    796.334092—dc22 [B]   2006038391

Manufactured in the United States of America
1 2 3 4 5 6 – JR – 12 11 10 09 08 07

Contents

Redemption

A penalty kick in a World Cup match is always a big deal. At that moment, a nation of soccer fans stops and holds its collective breath. But in the 2002 World Cup, the stakes for David Beckham were even higher. His country, England, was playing its most bitter rival, Argentina. David had a chance to make up for a horrible mistake he had made four years earlier. As he was about to step forward to strike the ball, David realized that his whole life had been leading up to this moment.

Until the 1998 World Cup in France, David had lived a charmed life. He was then only twenty-three years old but was already a soccer star. He was a member of Manchester United as well as England's national team. David had helped England qualify for the 1998 World Cup. He'd come from a close, stable family and was about to marry a world-famous pop star. None of this had prepared him for what was about to occur.

For David, disaster struck in the 1998 World Cup during England's second-round match against Argentina in Saint Etienne, France. The match was tied 2–2 early in the second half when Argentinean Diego Simeone, who was known for his unsporting behavior, kicked David from behind and tried to ruffle his hair. David shouldn't have taken the bait. He knew that Simeone was just trying to provoke him. But he reacted anyway. He kicked back. Even though he didn't make much contact, Simeone went down and the referee gave David a red card, which meant he could no longer play and couldn't be replaced. His mistake left England with ten players to Argentina's eleven—a huge disadvantage.

England went on to lose the match after extra time (overtime) and penalty kicks (which are used to settle matches that are still tied after 120 minutes). The blame, rightly or wrongly, fell squarely on David. Manager Glenn Hoddle, who had questioned David's maturity before the tournament, claimed that England would have won if they hadn't been down a man. Meanwhile, newspapers ran headlines such as TEN HEROIC LIONS, ONE STUPID BOY.

The criticism of David was intense. For a while, he escaped to the United States. When he returned to England, he needed a police escort to get through the airport. Reporters hounded him and his family. David was shocked by it all.

At one point, David's father suggested that he might have to go play soccer for a foreign team if the bad treatment continued. But he returned to his English team, Manchester United, and resurrected his career. He was a huge part of the United team that won every major trophy the next season—the English Premier League (EPL), the English FA Cup, and Europe's Champions League. He also kept his place on the national team and was even named captain in early 2001. Although he scored the vital goal that qualified England for the 2002 World Cup, he knew that he had only one way to make up for his mistake in 1998. He had to help England beat Argentina in the 2002 World Cup.

His chance came late in the first half of their first-round match. Italian referee Signor Collina awarded England a penalty kick. Normally, striker Michael Owen would have taken it. But as captain, David chose to take it himself. Not surprisingly, the Argentineans tried to unnerve him. David had never been under so much pressure. Simeone stood between him and the goal and walked toward him offering to shake his hand. David did his best to blank him out of his thoughts.

David decided not to try a fancy shot. He'd just bang the ball as hard as he could. "I was far too nervous to try to be clever," he said. David simply slammed the ball into the middle of the net, past the surprised goalkeeper.

He had finally fully redeemed himself. "The nerves, the pressure, and the four years of memories just fell away," he later wrote. "In those few seconds after the ball settled in the back of Argentina's net, I could see flashbulbs fire off around the ground. As each little explosion died against the blur and color of the stands, it took something that had happened, something that had been said or written since my red card in Saint Etienne, away into the night sky with it."

Chapter | One

His Dad and a Ball

David Beckham grew up dreaming of two things: becoming a professional soccer player and taking the field for Manchester United. His dad, Ted, inspired both of these dreams and did everything in his power to help make them come true.

David Robert Joseph Beckham was born on May 2, 1975, in Leytonstone, a neighborhood in London, England. His father, Ted, was a kitchen fitter (installer) and his mother, Sandra, was a hairdresser. David had an older sister, Lynne, who sometimes looked after him, and a younger sister named Joanne. Before he turned five, his family moved to Chingford, a suburb just outside London.

David had to do his share of chores while he was growing up. He had to set the table before supper, serve tea to guests when his mom took hairstyling appointments at home, and look after Joanne. But he spent most of his free time playing soccer.

His dad was his greatest source of encouragement. Ted had been a huge fan of Manchester United since 1958. The majority of the team had died in an airplane crash that year. Ted was far from alone in his devotion to the team. The sympathy the crash generated helped make Manchester United one of the most popular clubs in the world. Ted passed on that love to his son by giving him a replica jersey and taking him to see United play whenever the club came to London. It worked. By the time David was five, he told anyone who would listen that he would play for United someday.

THE 1958 TRAGEDY

In February 1958, twenty-three passengers, including eight Manchester United players and three club officials, died in a plane crash. The crash occurred during takeoff in Munich, Germany, after a 3–3 draw with Red Star Belgrade of Yugoslavia. The tragedy is generally considered to be one of the saddest days in English sporting history.

Ted had been a very good soccer player and had earned tryouts with professional clubs. He still played in organized leagues when David was a kid. As David remembers, Ted clearly wanted his son to follow in his footsteps. David had a ball to kick as soon as he could walk. Ted also practiced with him after he finished work and passed on all of his knowledge about the sport. Father and son started out playing in the back garden but had to move to nearby Chase Lane Park because David was ruining the flower bed by kicking the ball too hard.

Ted had strong opinions about what David needed to learn. Like any young player, David wanted to shoot rather than practice fundamentals. But Ted wouldn't indulge him. He taught David how to strike the ball equally well with either foot. Ted also kicked the ball as high as he could and taught David how to control it while it was coming down. And he encouraged his son to release the ball quickly, which would save him from suffering too many tackles. Father and son worked together hour after hour, until the sun set. Ted asked a lot from David, but his guidance helped David master the basics and taught him the value of developing good habits.

All the hard work quickly paid off. David was small for his age, but older kids often came to his house to invite David to play with them at Chase Lane Park. Ted also took him to play with grown men in five-a-side pickup matches at a sports and social club called Wadham Lodge. The fact that his dad rarely protected him on the field served him well in the long run. David learned to watch out for himself.

> **❝**[Dad] warned me that I had to be prepared to get a bit roughed up now and again. If he'd been running around telling people not to tackle me all evening, it would have been pointless me being there in the first place.**❞**
>
> —DAVID BECKHAM[6]

He also started practicing free kicks at Wadham Lodge. He could have done this at Chase Lane Park, but he preferred to work on what would become his trademark skill in front of his dad. David's mom was also a huge help. She drove David's teams to and from matches in a minibus and made sure that he had his uniform and all the right equipment.

David was clearly ready to take on the challenge of playing organized soccer, and opportunity soon knocked. According to his mom, Stuart Underwood knocked on the front door and asked the Beckhams whether seven-year-old David could join his team. Underwood coached Ridgeway Rovers, a youth club that played in the Enfield District League. David's dad, however, claims that they had sought out Underwood after coming across an advertisement that read, "Wanted: Football Stars of the Future." (Soccer is called football in most countries.)

ENGLAND'S LEAGUES

In England professional teams play in different leagues. The Premier League (also called the Premiership or the EPL) is the top league. Then comes the Championship, the First Division, the Second Division, and the Third Division. These groupings are somewhat like American professional baseball, where teams compete in the major leagues and several levels of minor leagues. One important difference is that the English clubs in the lower leagues are not affiliated with any Premier League club.

David still doesn't know which parent was right, but he has no doubts about how much playing for Underwood's Rovers helped him. Underwood was brutally honest with his players. He wasn't afraid to tell them exactly what they were doing wrong. David credits Underwood with playing a big part in preparing him for a career in soccer.

Underwood and his assistants, who included Ted Beckham, taught the boys how to play soccer and conduct themselves on the field. They worked in small groups so the players could get a lot of individual attention. The coaches stressed positional play and how to move without the ball. The children also learned that they could not play in matches unless they came to practice that week. They were expected to dress well before big matches—wearing collars and ties.

Several of David's teammates went on to professional careers. Micah Hyde played at Watford, Jason Brissett went to Bournemouth, and Chris Day, who played center forward with the Rovers, ended up tending goal for Queens Park Rangers. David, however, was the clear star of his team. In three seasons, he scored more than one hundred goals and began to attract serious attention from professional scouts.

In 1985, at age ten, David traveled to Manchester, a large city in central England, to enter the weeklong Bobby Charlton Soccer Skills Tournament. He was going to compete against other promising players, many of whom were much older than he. The competition was named after one of Manchester United's greatest players. David was not quite ready for such stiff competition, though. He didn't win. He felt lost and homesick during the tournament, and he had a toothache to boot.

 Bobby Charlton starred for England in the 1966 World Cup. That year was the first—and last—year that England won the World Cup. He also helped United win the European Cup in 1968.

David returned to the tournament in 1986. He competed against more than one hundred finalists who came from all over Great Britain and Ireland. He won the skills competition in front of forty thousand fans at Manchester United's stadium, Old Trafford. Charlton himself presented the trophy to David. David also won a trip to Barcelona, Spain. There he met Terry Venables, the manager of Futbol Club (FC) Barcelona, a Spanish professional team, and Gary Lineker, an Englishman who was the leading scorer in the 1986 World Cup. He also met Mark Hughes, who later transferred from Barcelona to Manchester United. It was a lot for an eleven-year-old to take in.

When David traveled to Barcelona in 1986, he made a big impression on Venables. "I was so impressed with the lad [boy] that I rang up my dad in London and told him to keep an eye on him," Venables said.

David was small and shy, but his skill and determination were evident. One opponent, Nana Boachie, still remembers his first encounter with David. "We were both eleven in our first proper football contest and David desperately wanted to start off with a goal," Boachie said. "As goalie on the opposing side,

I wanted to keep a clean sheet. He just said, 'We'll see,' in that quiet voice of his. Just before halftime, we gave away a free kick just outside the [penalty] area. David curled the ball into the top corner. It was impossible to save." (A free kick is awarded to a player when a member of the other team has committed a foul outside the penalty area. Free kicks are taken from the spot where the foul took place.)

David's teachers at Chingford spotted his potential as well. One evaluation described him as having "a natural ability to succeed in sports." He knew the basics and, as biographer Jimmy Burns explained, he "worked on them, with genuine enthusiasm for the game. He was football mad, and from an early age it was evident that the boy carried a drive within him that set him apart from the other kids who kicked the ball around in school games." (The word *mad* is British slang for "crazy.")

David was confident in his soccer skills. In fact, he later admitted that the only time he felt really sure of himself was when he was on the soccer field.

Chapter | Two

Dream Coming True

The English Premiership—the soccer league to which Manchester United belongs—does not have an amateur draft. Youngsters are free to start training with professional clubs at any age. Clubs can sign a player to a professional contract long before the player's eighteenth birthday.

At around age eleven, David was playing with Ridgeway Rovers and for various local all-star teams. He also started training with a small club called Leyton Orient (where his father had once tried out) and Tottenham Hotspur, a much bigger club located just fifteen miles away from his home in Chingford. Although he was flattered by the attention both clubs paid to him, his heart was still set on one club: Manchester United.

David had just finished playing what he remembers as one of his best matches when his mom approached him. "Lucky you

13

had a good game today," she said. "That man over there, he's a Man United scout. They want to have a look at you."

A range of emotions overwhelmed David. "I can still remember the rush of joy and excitement," he recalled. "There was relief in there too. I burst into tears on the spot, just cried and cried. I couldn't believe how happy I felt. I'd wondered for such a long time if I'd ever hear those words."

Manchester United's London scout, Malcolm Fidgeon, decided that David deserved a chance to try out for the club. He looked after David and even drove him to Manchester for a series of practice sessions. Despite the pressure, David loved staying in Manchester, especially since he got to play and talk about soccer all the time.

 Unlike the major team sports in the United States, soccer clubs can field players of any age.

David's skills and hard work must have made a good impression. The club wanted to sign him. One night the team's manager, Alex Ferguson, called the Beckham house and told Ted that David was just the kind of player and person they wanted to represent their club. Ted Beckham was understandably proud.

David later recalled his dad telling him, "He phoned to say they enjoyed meeting you, that you've got talent and they think your character is a credit to you, and to me and Mum. He said you're just the kind of boy Manchester United are looking for."

David wanted to sign with the club, but matters weren't quite that simple. Tottenham Hotspur also wanted him. The team had a lot to offer. Spurs, as the team was called, was his grandfather's favorite club. David's family and friends would be able to attend more matches because the club was in London. David also really liked working with the club's youth development officer, John Moncur. And Terry Venables, who was managing FC Barcelona when David visited that city, was now working at Spurs, which meant that David had a chance to be trained by someone with a world-class reputation.

Most important, he wanted the security that comes with signing a long-term contract. David dreamed of playing for United, but even at age thirteen he was already wise enough to realize that he had to look after his professional best interest. He and his dad decided that they should listen to offers from both clubs. And Ted made it clear that he would not try to sway David's opinion even though he hoped he would sign with United.

First, David met with Moncur and Venables at White Hart Lane, where Spurs is headquartered. Venables had been so impressed with David in Barcelona that he had asked his dad to keep an eye on him, but when they met this time, he asked Moncur, "So, John, what have you got to tell me about this young lad?" The question left David with the impression that Venables had no idea who he was, despite the fact that he had been training with the club for about two years.

Where the Boys Are

When teenage boys sign with professional soccer clubs such as Manchester United, they don't immediately become a member of the first team, or senior squad. Instead they play for the club's youth team. The oldest players on youth teams are eighteen or nineteen years old. United's youth team plays in the FA Premier Academy League against other teams of young prospects. One of the top tournaments for youth teams is the FA Youth Cup.

Between the youth team and the first team is the reserve team. England's top reserve team league is the FA Premier Reserve League, and United's reserve team plays in this league. A player may spend a year or more on the reserve team before getting the chance to play for the first team.

This contrasted sharply with the impression Alex Ferguson had made during David's practice sessions at Manchester United. David couldn't stop thinking about his time at

Manchester. Ferguson knew and cared about every boy. David felt like he was part of a family there.

Still, Spurs wasn't out of the running, especially since the club offered David a generous six-year contract. The thought of all the money he would make by signing made him daydream about owning a Porsche by the time he turned eighteen. On the way to Manchester, David and his dad made an effort to put thoughts of money aside. They wanted to be assured that David would get a fair chance to prove himself.

Manchester United was playing against Wimbledon that day in May 1989. Unlike Venables, Ferguson couldn't have been more personable. The club presented David with a red club tie, treated him to lunch in the grill room, where the players had their prematch meals, and even presented him with a cake to celebrate his fourteenth birthday. After the match, David and his dad met with Ferguson, Fidgeon, and Les Kershaw, who was in charge of youth development. Ferguson offered him a six-year contract, just like Spurs had. David hadn't heard all the details, but that didn't stop him from saying that he wanted to sign.

The club's official announcement about the signing was slightly more subdued: "David is a good prospect. We are delighted that he is joining us."

Signing for a club is one thing, making the grade with it quite another. David had to move away from home and compete, day after day, against other talented boys. David had some advantages—his ball skills and stamina—but the real secret to his success was hard work. Looking back, he realizes the extent to which he avoided all the temptations that come with being a teenager. "I gave up a lot when I was younger, going out with the lads, parties and discos, leaving my family," he recalled. "It wasn't easy, but I knew it was what I wanted to do."

In the early 1990s, David was lucky to have a brilliant youth coach, Eric Harrison, who helped him and several other Manchester United players become stars. Harrison believed that a good coach was like a good teacher. "They realize the youngsters are the important ones," he said. "We do it for the kids, not for our own egos. I have taken so much pleasure from seeing young players develop both as footballers [soccer players] and people." He helped nurture Ryan Giggs, Nicky Butt, Paul Scholes, and Gary and Phil Neville, among others, but he was particularly proud of his pupil from Chingford. "David might have funny haircuts and live a different life from the rest of us, but the important thing is, he's a really good kid," he later said.

The respect was mutual. David considers Harrison one of the three most important influences on his soccer career, along with his dad and Ferguson. In fact, he still calls Harrison for advice. David appreciates Harrison's honesty. His old coach tells him the truth, even when David doesn't want to hear it.

Setting the Rules

The formal rules for the game of soccer were established on December 8, 1863, at a tavern in London. But there was disagreement over whether players should be allowed to use their hands and tackle opponents rather than the ball. From these disagreements, two groups split off. One group created the rules for soccer (in which players couldn't use their hands and could tackle only the ball). A second group eventually created the rules for rugby, which allows players to do both.

Harrison had a fierce reputation, which David thought was fully deserved. The coach became angry if his players made mistakes. On the other hand, praise from him made David feel satisfied. One compliment could make his whole day. Harrison made his players work and practice hard. But he also understood them as people as well as players. Two of his most important contributions to David's game were making him play the ball with his head more and getting him to make more tackles.

Everyone's hard work began to pay off in 1992. Harrison's team beat Spurs to advance to the 1992 FA Youth Cup Final. The team's opponent was Crystal Palace. The first of two matches took place at Palace, on a wet field. Manchester United won 3–1.

Butt scored twice, and David found the net with a left-footed volley from the edge of the box. The win meant that United needed only to avoid being beaten by more than one goal to capture the Youth Cup. United went on to win 3–2 in the second game in front of 32,000 fans at Old Trafford. The Cup triumph made it clear that this group of players, which became known as Fergie's Fledglings in honor of their manager, was special.

BABES AND FLEDGLINGS

In the 1950s, Manchester United manager Matt Busby nurtured a talented group of young players, including Bobby Charlton. That group was called Busby's Babes. In a similar fashion, the class of 1992 became known as Fergie's Fledglings.

Bobby Charlton, who had led Manchester United to the top of European soccer in 1968, gushed about their quality. "I've never known us—or any club in England—to have so many potentially brilliant youngsters," he said.

Even the cautious Ferguson predicted that his fledglings had a bright future. "We don't like to go overboard about young players, but this lot are very exciting. With their ability and desire to play, they should go far. Winning the FA Youth Cup can be significant. When United last won it in 1964, it triggered the best period in the club's recent history." The class of 1964 went on to win the English First Division in 1965 and 1967 and the European Cup in 1968. Charlton and Ferguson believed that the class of 1992 could be just as successful.

 The European Cup, which Manchester United won in 1968, has since been renamed the Champions League. Meanwhile, the First Division has been renamed the Premiership.

Chapter | Three

Moving Up

Having so much success at the youth level could have gone to David's head, but his dad had already taken steps to prevent that from happening. After his son agreed to commit his future to Manchester United, Ted warned him not to get carried away. "You may have signed for Man United, but you haven't done anything yet," Ted told his son. "When you've played for the first team, then we can talk about you having achieved something. Until then, don't start thinking you've made it."

After the 1992 FA Youth Cup triumph, David and many of his young teammates appeared to be on the way to establishing themselves with the senior (main) squad. In September of that same year, Ferguson promoted Gary Neville, Nicky Butt, Paul Scholes, and David for a League Cup match against Brighton. Compared to other competitions, the League Cup isn't very important. It ranks fourth in importance behind the English Premier League, the FA Cup, and the Champions League, which pits the best clubs from each country against one another. Still, playing for the senior club at age seventeen seemed to signal that David's time was about to come.

SOCCER POSITIONS

Soccer has four types of positions. The goalkeeper is the only player who is allowed to use the hands. Defenders help to defend the goal. Central defenders usually play in front of the goalkeeper, while fullbacks cover the area near the sidelines. The attackers are also called strikers or forwards. These players are supposed to score most of the team's goals. The final group is the midfielders. These players alternate between attacking and defending. Some midfielders, such as David, usually play near the sideline, while others play in the middle. In all, a team may have eleven players on the field.

Ferguson put in David as a substitute with seventeen minutes remaining. David was so excited that he banged his head on the roof of the dugout when the manager told him to go in. He calmed down and afterward felt that he had played all right.

Apparently Ferguson wasn't nearly so pleased. He yelled at David in front of his teammates after the match. David had to play two more years with the reserve team before the manager gave him another chance with the senior side.

David played in some more League Cup matches in the 1994–1995 season, and Ferguson started him against Galatasaray from Turkey in the Champions League in December 1994. The match wasn't as glamorous as most European Cup matches because Manchester United had already been mathematically eliminated from the championship. But it was still a big opportunity for David. This time he took full advantage by scoring his first goal for United on the way to a 4–0 win. Ferguson must have been pleased. He didn't say anything to his young star after the match.

That start, however, raised false hopes. In early 1995, David found himself back on the reserve team and was then told that he was going to be loaned out to a small club called Preston North End. The change made David very nervous. Many players are loaned to small clubs before being sold to them. He feared that he was being farmed out to a small club because the coaching staff at Manchester United had decided that he wasn't good enough to play for them.

David thought the message was clear. His longtime teammates Gary Neville and Nicky Butt were already getting plenty of action with the first team. David felt like he was lagging behind. He was worried that United was ready to give up on him.

❝I knew [David] was worried [about being loaned to Preston]. He thought that was the end of him at United. We all knew he had great ability but people said he was a bit soft going into tackles and headers.❞

—GARY NEVILLE

Ferguson met with David to make it clear that United had no intention of showing him the door. The boss just wanted him to have a chance to play regularly in another league.

The conversation with Ferguson helped David arrive in Preston in a more positive frame of mind. But he still had a major adjustment to make. Preston played in the Third Division of the English League, which is similar to playing single-A minor-league baseball in the United States. There weren't many frills. After his first practice, David threw his dirty uniform on the ground, expecting the cleaning staff to wash it. He was quickly told to take it home and wash it by the next day.

David had no problem doing his own laundry, but he was concerned about how rough the play in the Third Division could be. As he watched the physical play from the bench in his first game, he found himself cringing at the hard tackles and dreading the moment he would take the field. But despite his nerves, he played well once he got into the game in the second half. He even set up a goal with a corner kick. (A corner kick is awarded when the defending team lays the ball out of bounds behind their own goal line. A member of the offensive team then takes a free kick from the corner closest to where the ball went out of bounds.)

In his second match, against Fulham, David was still worried about the rough play. Fulham had a player named Terry Hurlock who had a reputation as a fierce tackler. David wasn't looking forward to the encounter, but he discovered, perhaps to his own surprise, that he could handle such rough play. "I was worried about getting whacked by [Hurlock]," he admitted. "As it turned out, I didn't and got a few challenges in myself. You soon realize that . . . you can't afford to be ducking out of the physical side."

 Fulham, one of David's Third Division opponents, is currently a member of the Premier League. English teams get promoted to the next-highest league if they finish among the top teams in the standings. Meanwhile, they are sent to the next-lowest league if they finish among the bottom three.

Preston got the three points that come with a win (a team receives one point for a draw). It won 3–2, and David converted his first free kick in a professional match. One of his teammates celebrated by grabbing his head and pulling his hair. That hurt so much that it overshadowed the goal itself.

The intensity of that celebration and the way Preston players gave everything they had in every match impressed David. The players didn't make big money like those playing with the major clubs. They were playing to scratch out a living, and that gave the game an intensity David had never experienced.

David had such an exciting time during his month at Preston that he asked Ferguson to let him stay when Manchester United recalled him. The boss turned down David's request without offering any explanation.

He got something far better than an explanation. Ferguson selected him to start the next match against one of the better teams in the EPL, Leeds United. He realized that the boss's decision to loan him out had prepared him to play for United. Playing for Preston had helped him bring his game to a new level.

❝ *Going to the Third Division with Preston and having people kick lumps out [of David] toughened him up.* ❞
—GARY NEVILLE

The Manchester United game ended 0–0, but nineteen-year-old David did well enough to earn a few more starts in EPL matches before the end of the season. He felt like he had turned a corner. His dad's advice about achievement proved to be right on the mark. He was a regular starter for Manchester United, and he had every right to feel like he had achieved something.

Chapter Four

Youth Is Served

English soccer is run very differently from the major professional team sports in the United States. In the United States, the purpose of the regular season is to determine who will qualify for the playoffs, and the team that wins the playoff tournament is crowned champion. Most countries, like England, where soccer is the major sport, don't have a playoff system. Instead, each team plays against every other team twice, home and away. The team with the most points is awarded the EPL championship.

At the same time, all the professional teams in a country, from the EPL all the way down to the small regional leagues, compete in a single-elimination tournament called the FA Cup. This competition is much less predictable. Opponents are determined through a random draw. A club such as Manchester United might have to play an away match against a club from a smaller league, such as Preston North End. The winner advances, and a new random draw takes place to see who will face off in the next round. This process continues until only two teams are left to play in the FA Cup Final.

The other major difference is that the best English clubs compete against the best clubs from other European countries in a continent-wide competition. The most prestigious tournament is called the Champions League. It is played over the same time period as the other competitions. This means that Manchester United enters every season competing for three major trophies. Any season in which the team doesn't win at least one trophy is considered a disappointment.

Under the guidance of Ferguson, Manchester United had become the most successful club in England. The team won the EPL in 1993 for the first time in twenty-six years. It won the EPL and the FA Cup in 1994, which the English refer to as doing the Double. But United failed to win any trophies in the 1994–1995 season. It was eliminated in an early stage of the Champions League, finished second by one point to Blackburn Rovers in the EPL, and lost the FA Cup Final 1–0 to Everton. These results might have been good enough for most clubs, but Ferguson decided that his team needed some changes.

Ferguson transferred three players who had played a huge part of United's recent success—forward Mark Hughes, midfielder

Paul Ince, and Andrei Kanchelskis, an attacking right-sided midfielder. This was good news for David and many of his teammates who had played together on United's youth team. Ferguson was ready to give them greater responsibilities. Gary Neville started at right fullback, while his brother Phil became a valuable utility player who could play either in defense or midfield. Paul Scholes and Nicky Butt competed to replace Ince and start next to Roy Keane in the center of midfield. Ryan Giggs had already established himself on the left side of midfield. And David took over for Kanchelskis on the right.

Fans often refer to Manchester United as the Red Devils. For home games, the players wear red shirts, white shorts, and black socks. The color of their road uniforms varies from year to year. Unlike U.S. sports teams, English clubs do not usually wear any traditional colors when they are playing away.

Ferguson felt confident about David's role with Manchester United. "I was reassured with Beckham's promise," said the manager. "He was a late developer but was coming into the reckoning and although I wasn't sure whether he would be operating wide or in central midfield, he was certain to be an increasingly important member of the squad."

No one doubted that this group was talented, but critics wondered whether Ferguson had gone too far, especially after United lost its first match of the season 3–1 to Aston Villa. Had he overreacted to one disappointing season? Was it wise to make so many changes so quickly? Would this team prove to be too young and too inexperienced?

After the defeat by Villa, Alan Hanson, one of the most famous soccer commentators in the country, told a national television audience that he thought Ferguson was making a terrible blunder. "You can't win anything with kids," Hanson said. David had scored United's only goal, but on the bus ride back to Manchester, even he wondered whether he and his young teammates were ready.

Ferguson, however, kept faith in his youngsters. They won their next match, 2–1, at home against West Ham United and went on to win five straight. The most important victory was a match against defending EPL champion Blackburn. The score was tied 1–1 when David pounced on a loose ball just outside the penalty area. He curled it into the upper right-hand corner of the net. The goal, which won the match, was huge for him and the club and made the players and fans think that United had a chance to win the EPL.

In January United was in second place but trailed Newcastle United by twelve points. At this point, the FA Cup competition started. United drew a relatively small club called Sunderland at home, but could do no better than a 2–2 draw. The two teams had to play again, this time at Sunderland. United fell behind after twenty-four minutes, but Scholes tied the score in the seventieth minute. Andy Cole's goal won the match in the eighty-ninth minute. Dramatic wins like that often inspire a team. Such was the case with United. They beat Reading, a small club, 3–0 in the next round of the FA Cup and also closed the gap on Newcastle to just four points by February 18.

Newcastle is a city in northeastern England on the Tyne River. Newcastle United formed in 1892, when two local clubs joined together. The club has won the FA Cup six times and the EPL four times, although it has never won both in the same year.

Although David was proud of the role that he and his fellow fledglings were playing for United, he felt that a core group of veterans deserved even more credit. The club's Danish goalkeeper, Peter Schmeichel, was probably the best in the world. David thought that the intensity with which he practiced sharpened the skills of all the players, especially the attackers. Roy Keane was the driving force behind the team on the field. If a player made a mistake, he could be sure that Keane would give him an earful. David came to realize that the verbal bashings weren't personal. "It doesn't matter to Roy if you've been playing for United for ten years or just ten games," he said. "If he thinks he needs to, he'll hammer you. It's all about wanting to win."

The biggest influence on the team, however, was a Frenchman named Eric Cantona. The fact that he was suspended (for kicking a fan) for the first six weeks of the season goes a long way toward explaining why United fell twelve points behind Newcastle. Cantona rarely spoke to David about soccer, but that didn't stop David from trying to copy everything he did. He was the joker in United's deck—a creative and completely unpredictable presence on the field. Twenty-year-old David came to realize that one of the biggest reasons for Cantona's success was sheer hard work. After the team practiced, Cantona would go off and train on his own. He worked on his fundamentals, doing many of the same training exercises that David had started doing with his dad at age seven.

Cantona scored goal after vital goal for United. He scored the first goal in their fifth-round FA Cup victory over bitter rival Manchester City. Next he scored the only goal in the club's win away at Newcastle, which lifted United to first place in the EPL. And then he scored the winner in United's FA Cup quarterfinal victory against Southampton.

 The FA Cup began in 1871. Wanderers beat Royal Engineers 1–0 in the first Final.

United's opponent in the FA Cup semifinal was Chelsea, one of the bigger clubs from London. The Blues, as the team is known, scored first, but Andy Cole tied it at one. The match was tense when one of Chelsea's defenders misplayed a ball. David raced in and knocked the ball forward with his shin. The ball bounced wider of the goal than he probably would have liked, but he slotted it past the advancing keeper into the far corner of the net. His tally proved to be the winner. David was so emotional that he began to cry after he looked up and saw his mom and dad sitting in the stands.

Meanwhile, Manchester United held a lead over Newcastle for the EPL crown. David and his teammates needed to win their final game of the season at Middlesbrough to clinch the title. They may have still been young, but by this point they could handle the pressure. They won 3–0. David May scored after just fifteen minutes, and Cole and Giggs wrapped up the match in the second half.

The quality of the team's play during the title chase left David in a slight state of shock. "We'd just kept coming in for training, turning up for games and were all on the kind of high which has you half expecting things to go wrong at any minute. In the United first team? Winning the Premiership? There had to be a catch. But there wasn't. Instead, it got better and better."

Like most English boys, David had dreamed of playing in an FA Cup Final at Wembley Stadium in London. It's more important to win the EPL, but the FA Cup has always held a special place with players and fans. Part of its allure stems from the fact that it is the oldest soccer competition in the world. The Final is also popular because it used to be the only domestic game that was broadcast live on TV during the entire season. This was the one match that every soccer fan got to watch.

Manchester United's opponent was Liverpool, one of the best teams in England and one of United's biggest rivals. Fans on both sides had great expectations, but the match started slowly. It was still goalless late in the second half. Both teams were too scared of each other to take any risks. David wasn't as sharp as usual, and Ferguson considered substituting for him because his corner kicks had been so poor. But Ferguson stuck with him. With one minute to go, David set up to take one last corner. He swung the ball in just outside the six-yard box. David James, Liverpool's goalkeeper, managed to get a hand to it and knock it just outside the penalty box. James appeared to have done just enough, but somehow Cantona read the flight of the ball and volleyed it back into the Liverpool goal.

A GAME FOR EVERYONE

The FA Cup Final used to be the only domestic soccer game shown in its entirety on English television. Most matches were shown on two highlight shows. *Match of the Day* was broadcast late on Saturday night and the *Big Match* aired on Sunday. The owners of the clubs were reluctant to televise live matches because they thought that fans would lose interest in attending matches in person.

David felt that the goal celebration that followed was a fitting way to end such an improbable season. "I think the whole team got to Eric [Cantona] inside a split second and it seemed like he lifted the lot of us off the ground and carried us back to the halfway line. It was the story of the whole fantastic season, right there." Against all odds, Fergie's Fledglings had done the Double.

Chapter Five

A Star Is Made

Sometimes achieving something too quickly can do more harm than good. Early success can make a player feel too satisfied or fool a team into believing that future success is assured. David Beckham was not about to let that happen to him.

"You cannot afford to let things go to your head," he explained. "First of all you'd get hammered by the other lads, then you have to face up to the boss. The first sign that you're getting carried away and he comes down like a ton of bricks. I know how difficult it's been just breaking into the first team and I'm not going to do anything to put that at risk. . . . I would be stupid to think I'm something special."

Manchester United began the 1996–1997 EPL season by beating Wimbledon 3–0. The win showed that complacency wasn't a concern. The match will always be remembered for one moment. In the final minute, Brian McClair made a simple pass to David just inside United's half of the field. Normally a player would just hold the ball or make another simple pass, but David took a shot instead. He couldn't hear Ferguson but later was told that his boss just growled, "What does he think he's trying now?"

Ferguson would soon find out. The ball looked like it was going to go out of bounds between the goal and the corner flag, but David had bent it. The ball stayed in the air and swerved over Wimbledon goalkeeper Neil Sullivan's head into the net.

It may have been only the first match, but no one doubted that David had scored what would prove to be the goal of the season. After the match, everyone except Ferguson heaped praise on him. Ted Beckham hugged him. Eric Cantona came over to congratulate him, and people on the street kept coming up to offer praise. David's life would never be the same. With that amazing goal, he had become a star.

One month later, in September, David was called to represent England for the first time. He'd be playing for his country in a World Cup qualifying match. The team's new manager, Glenn Hoddle, didn't call to inform him. Instead, David found out while he was watching TV with his mom. He was elated. Representing one's country is among the highest honors any player can receive. David jumped off the sofa and hugged his mom. He called his dad at work to share the good news.

Even Ferguson congratulated and encouraged him. "If you get the chance, play well," he advised his star. "Just play like you have been doing for us at United."

Hoddle had praised David as a player who "sees the furthest pass first," but there was no guarantee that David would start or even play as a substitute. England was preparing to play a World Cup qualifier against Moldova. David didn't expect Hoddle to play someone who didn't already have international experience. But David practiced so well that the England boss selected him to start. That choice turned out to be wise. The field was bumpy, slowing down the play, but England still left the field as 3–0 winners. David helped set up the first and last goals. He felt that he played well enough to keep his place on the team.

> The number of teams from each continent to qualify for the World Cup varies. Fourteen teams from Europe qualified for the 2006 World Cup. Meanwhile, only four, including the United States, qualified from the region that consists of North America, Central America, and the Caribbean (called CONCACAF).

Hoddle must have been satisfied too. He selected David to play in every qualifying match for the 1998 World Cup in France.

Qualifying for the finals is a long, drawn-out process. Teams from each continent are divided into groups. In Europe, only the teams that finish at the top of their groups are guaranteed a place in the World Cup.

England's most difficult opponent was Italy. England needed to get at least a tie against Italy in the last match, in Rome, to secure its place in France. Italy had won its last fifteen matches in Rome, and most experts felt that England was the underdog. But Hoddle devised a brilliant game plan. Italy was famous for playing cautiously, but England tried to beat the Italians at their own game. England maintained possession for long spells but was careful not to send too many players forward. This forced the Italians to use their energy chasing the ball. The strategy frustrated the Italians to the point that one of their players, Angelo di Livio, received a red card.

 Italy has won the World Cup four times, in 1934, 1938, 1982, and 2006.

With a few minutes to go, it looked like England had earned the draw it needed. In fact, Ian Wright nearly won the match for the team, but his shot bounced off the post. Right away the Italians got the ball up to the other end. All of England's hard work was at risk. Christian Vieri had a free header in the England box, a chance he would usually make, but his shot went wide. The referee blew the whistle a few seconds later to signal the end of the match. England's players and coaching staff raced onto the field to begin a wild, relief-filled celebration. They would be playing in the World Cup in the summer of 1998.

The commitment required to play for his country didn't get in the way of David's obligations to his club. Manchester United had a stellar season in 1996–1997. The team put together a sixteen-match unbeaten streak and finished seven points ahead of Newcastle. United had won its fourth championship in five years, and the future looked bright with Fergie's Fledglings coming into their prime. But the club would have to face it without Cantona, who announced his retirement at the end of the season.

Manchester United's season wasn't perfect, though. The team was eliminated in the fourth round of the FA Cup at Wimbledon, and it lost to Borussia Dortmund of Germany in the semifinals of the Champions League. The failure against Dortmund was especially hard to take. United had accomplished so much in England, but it wouldn't get full credit for being a great club unless it won Europe's most prestigious competition. Still, David was pleased. United had won another major trophy, and the twenty-two-year-old was voted England's Young Player of the Year.

The Champions League, which was originally called the European Cup, began in 1955. The original format allowed only the champion from each nation to participate. It was renamed the Champions League in the 1990s. As many as four teams from a country may enter.

Not much came between David and soccer until he met a woman named Victoria Adams. Saying it was love at first sight might be an exaggeration, but only because they were already infatuated with each other before they ever met in person. She had seen a picture of him and asked, "Who's he? He's lovely." And then she went on to ask, "Is he famous?"

David didn't have to ask whether Victoria was famous. She went by the stage name Posh Spice in the Spice Girls, the well-known pop group. The first time he'd ever seen her was while he and Gary Neville were watching a video of the group before United played in a Champions League match in Tbilisi, Georgia. Victoria clearly made quite an impression. David had pointed to the TV and told his friend, "That is the girl for me and I am going to get her." He was right. They met after a Manchester United match. He asked her out and she accepted. Soon their relationship was serious.

The 1997–1998 season may have been kind to David's romantic life, but it was hard on Manchester United. The team was upset in the FA Cup by a small club called Barnsley and was eliminated from the Champions League by Monaco in the quarterfinals. Arsenal overtook United to claim the EPL crown. The team could have blamed its struggles on the retirement of Cantona or a knee injury that sidelined Roy Keane for most of the season. But that wouldn't have done justice to Arsenal, who captured the EPL by winning ten straight matches, including a crucial victory over United at Old Trafford. Arsenal then proved its superiority by beating Newcastle to win the FA Cup.

David has spread his wings beyond soccer. He's interested in fashion and even has his own bottled scent (cologne) called David Beckham Instinct.

Before the 1996–1997 season, Arsenal had hired a French manager named Arsene Wenger. He specialized in identifying and developing young talent, and his teams succeeded by playing entertaining, attack-minded soccer. Fergie's Fledglings were just coming into their prime, but the 1997–1998 season served notice that Manchester United had a new rival for the honor of being the best team in the land.

Chapter Six

More Than Redemption

After David received his infamous red card against Argentina in the 1998 World Cup, Manchester United showed it still believed in him, despite all the criticism he had received from the English press and public. United signed him to a new five-year contract, and Ferguson made it clear that the club stood behind him. "We will be looking after the player and we will protect him, because that is the way Manchester United behave," he said.

David was grateful for the way that the boss made him feel like he was part of a family. "Knowing he was behind me really helped me get through that summer in 1998, and the early part of the season that followed," he said. That kind of support helped David get through a difficult time in his career. But he knew that the best way he could silence his critics was on the playing field.

After David's red card in the 1998 World Cup, the anger against him was intense. One newspaper even printed a dartboard with his photo in the center.

The first match of the EPL season was against Leicester City at Old Trafford. The home fans got behind David and stood up to cheer every time he prepared to take a corner kick. The fan support meant a lot to him, but as the match was drawing to a close, United was still trailing by a goal. David had one last chance to salvage a tie as he stepped up to take a free kick just outside Leicester's penalty area. A hush came over the crowd. One thought kept running through David's mind: "Please go in. Please go in."

David struck the ball with the inside of his right foot. It spun up over the wall (a group of defenders standing close together), past the stunned goalkeeper, and settled into the corner of the goal. Excited, David ran to the corner flag with his arms outstretched and turned toward the fans. He felt so grateful for their support that he dedicated the game-tying goal to them.

United's next EPL match was at West Ham, which is in London, where David was born. The hostility directed at him was so threatening that he wondered if soccer was really worth such abuse. The match ended 0–0, but David learned that he could cope with difficult fans. The harsh treatment didn't end there, he later said, but that was when it stopped affecting him as a player.

The club responded to the adversity, led by its star. By January, United had qualified for the second round of the Champions League and was in the thick of the hunt for the Premiership. The team also won its third-round FA Cup match against Middlesbrough but found itself in deep trouble during its fourth-round match with Liverpool. Michael Owen scored for Liverpool early in the match. Try as they might, the United players could not create any meaningful chances for the next eighty minutes. Then Ferguson brought on a Norwegian striker named Ole Gunnar Solskjaer, who scored two quick goals to steal the match.

The next big challenge came in the quarterfinals of the Champions League. United had to play Internazionale of Italy—Diego Simeone's team. David knew he had to come to terms with the Argentinean who had successfully provoked him in France. They shook hands before the kickoff and exchanged jerseys afterward, but they didn't come into contact often during play. United prevailed 2–0, and David received a lot of praise for setting up two goals to Dwight Yorke with arrowlike crosses.

66[Beckham] is truly gifted. . . . If you want to win a major European trophy and show class along the way, you must play attacking football and he is ideal for an attacking formation. . . . He is a fabulous crosser of the ball and possesses terrific skill.99

—SOCCER GREAT JOHAN CRUYFF

The win would have been reason enough to celebrate, but David had something even more important to be proud about. Victoria gave birth to their son, Brooklyn, shortly after the match. Holding his son was a powerful experience for the twenty-three-year-old David. He later said that nothing in his life, on or off the soccer field, compared to it.

Caring for an infant is exhausting under the best of circumstances, but the success United was enjoying made it even more difficult for David. No English team had ever won the EPL, the FA Cup, and the Champions League in the same season, but United had a chance to win what the English call the Treble. By April, the club led Arsenal by a few points in the EPL. The two clubs also had to play each other in the semifinals of the FA Cup. The first match ended 0–0, which meant the clubs had to play again.

David had never scored against Arsenal, but early in the match he collected a loose ball outside the area and beat goaltender David Seaman (one of his teammates on England's national team). Arsenal later tied it with a goal from Dutch star Dennis Bergkamp. Roy Keane received a red card a few minutes later. United tried to dig in, but Arsenal's one-man advantage soon paid off. Arsenal drew a penalty kick in the closing minutes of the match. David was resigned to United's fate. He knew Bergkamp rarely missed penalty kicks. But somehow Peter Schmeichel dived to his left and saved it. The amazing save forced the match into an additional thirty minutes of extra time.

With about ten minutes to go in extra time, Arsenal's Patrick Vieira gave away the ball near the halfway line. Ryan Giggs gathered the ball and raced toward the Arsenal goal. Most players would have passed the ball, but Giggs just kept beating defenders until only Seaman stood in his way. He could have (and probably should have) passed the ball across the six-yard box to a teammate, but instead he whacked it past Seaman high on the near post side. It was the goal of a lifetime in one of the most exciting games of the year.

After the final whistle blew, Manchester United supporters rushed onto the field and hoisted some players, including David, onto their shoulders. David felt helpless, but he did manage to make a request: "While you've got me up here on your shoulders, could we try and head over towards where the dressing rooms are?"

The players barely had time to come down to earth. Their next key match was against Juventus of Turin, Italy, in the semifinals of the Champions League. United managed only to draw the first match 1–1 at Old Trafford, which meant that it had to win in Turin or score two or more goals if the match ended in a draw (due to a complicated tiebreaking system). Juventus had played in three of the previous four Champions League finals and went two goals ahead within the first ten minutes. United's hopes of doing the Treble seemed dim.

In 1977 Liverpool came within one match of winning the Treble but lost to Manchester United 2–1 in the the FA Cup Final.

Still David sensed that the team believed. He told Gary Neville, "They're not that good. . . . We can win this, you know." Midway through the first half, David took a corner kick and Keane headed the ball home. United's conviction grew. Yorke tied the match at 2–2 before the half, which was enough to qualify the club for the final if the score didn't change. Andy Cole made sure United advanced to the final by scoring the winner in the second half. The spirit of the team made the players feel unbeatable.

Breaking the Ties

With the exception of the Final, most pivotal Champions League matches are played over two legs. If one team wins both matches or wins one and ties the other, it advances to the next round. But matters become more complicated if the teams each win a match or if both matches end in draws. The first tiebreaker is total goals. But if that is the same, the team that scored the most goals away wins. For example, if Manchester United won 2–1 at home but lost 1–0 away, it would lose. If the teams are still deadlocked, a penalty shootout determines the winner.

United kept getting results, and the team soon found itself within three matches of doing the Treble. The first match, which could clinch the Premiership, was against Tottenham, the club David had spurned when he signed for United. Some fans and reporters thought that Spurs would not play hard because they didn't want their hated rival Arsenal to have a chance to claim the title (a United loss would help Arsenal). But that theory was laid to rest after Les Ferdinand opened the scoring for Spurs in the first half. The United players looked nervous and blew some easy chances, but David blasted a shot into the top corner before halftime. That settled their nerves, and Cole dribbled around Spurs' keeper to score the goal that secured United's fifth EPL title in seven years.

By comparison, the FA Cup Final against Newcastle was relatively uneventful. United played well and ran out comfortable 2–0 winners. Normally finishing off the Double would have kicked off a big celebration, but the Champions League Final against Bayern Munich, a German team, was just four days away. The team had to stay focused.

Because Keane and Paul Scholes had both been suspended for receiving too many yellow cards, Ferguson started David in the center of midfield next to Nicky Butt rather than in his customary position on the right. He also moved Giggs from the left side of midfield to David's normal position and put in Jesper Blomqvist to play on the left.

This may have been United's best lineup under the circumstances, but the players had not been playing as well as in recent weeks. They missed Keane's toughness and drive, and they had a noticeable lack of width, which meant the forwards, Cole and Yorke, were not getting served up as many cross passes as normal. Mario Basler scored for Bayern from a free kick after just six minutes, and the Germans came close to putting the match out of reach several times. Schmeichel made a couple of great saves to keep United in the game. Mehmet Scholl hit the post, and

Carsten Jancker's overhead kick hit the bar before rebounding into Schmeichel's arms with just six minutes left.

The only thing United had going for it was its never-say-die attitude, but hard work alone wasn't going to do the trick. The assistant official held up a sign indicating that there would be just three minutes of injury time (time added to the end of regulation to make up for stoppages in play due to injuries). United earned a corner kick, and David prepared to take what might be the team's last chance of the match. Schmeichel had moved forward into Bayern's penalty area, and David just wanted to place the ball in a dangerous spot.

In soccer, official time is not kept on a scoreboard. Only the referee knows when the match will end. The referee may blow the final whistle as soon as the amount of time added for injuries has been played. But he also has the right to let the match continue as long as he sees fit.

He floated it in successfully. Bayern's Stefan Effenberg hooked it away, but only as far as Giggs. Even though Giggs miskicked his shot, the ball bounced to Teddy Sheringham, who redirected the ball past Bayern's keeper, Oliver Kahn. All the

United players just went crazy, and David admitted later that he felt like crying. Somehow they had done it. It appeared that the game was moving on to thirty minutes of extra time.

Or would it? Two minutes remained, and Ferguson was screaming at the players to attack. They did and quickly won another corner kick. This time David—who was as excited as the United fans, who were singing and jumping up and down— kicked the ball toward the near post. Sheringham redirected the ball with his head across the box to Solskjaer, who stuck out his right foot and stabbed the ball into the far corner of the net. Goal! After the goal, Bayern got the ball back and kicked it straight to the United penalty box. For a moment, David was worried. But a United defender booted the ball away, and the referee blew the whistle to end the match. United had achieved the Treble!

The United players went wild. Some of them collapsed to the ground. Others, including David, ran around the field hugging one another. The magazine *World Soccer* called it the most dramatic Final ever. It was an amazing way to end a most remarkable season. David had more than redeemed himself.

Chapter Seven

One David Beckham

The summer of 1999 proved to be nearly as exciting as the 1998–1999 season. David and Victoria got married on July 4 in a fancy ceremony. The wedding took place in an Irish castle. Only close friends and family members were invited to the ceremony, but more than 340 guests, including Bobby Charlton and most of the Spice Girls, attended the reception.

David and Victoria were both very comfortable with being celebrities. They knew full well that their marriage, which many in Great Britain dubbed the Wedding of the Decade, was bound to make them even more famous. The couple also clearly has a taste for the finer things in life—food, clothes, and cars—but they say their family is more important to them than an expensive lifestyle. What's more, David has never let his celebrity status get in the way of his commitment to being a soccer player.

After a brief honeymoon in the south of France, David returned to Manchester United for preseason training. The players, who felt almost invincible, took up right where they had left off the previous season. United cruised through the opening group stage of the Champions League and trailed Leeds by just one point with two games in hand (two games more than Leeds had remaining) at the end of 1999.

The real drama for David during the fall centered around England's struggles to qualify for the 2000 European Football Championship (also called the European Championship). The national team was having problems both on and off the field. Manager Glenn Hoddle had been fired after he made insensitive remarks about disabled people. The team managed to finish second in its qualifying group, which meant that England had to play Scotland, first away and then at home, to decide who would move on to the Final.

The rivalry between the English and the Scottish teams was once intense. But the intensity is no longer what it used to be because the quality of Scotland's soccer team has declined. Still, matches between the teams are always passionate. These two matches were no exception. Paul Scholes scored twice for England in the first match at Glasgow, Scotland. The final score was England 2, Scotland 0. The loss should have all but eliminated the Scots.

England, Scotland, Wales, and Northern Ireland are considered separate countries in soccer. They are all part of Great Britain but are treated as individual countries to honor the fact that the game was invented in England.

During the second game, at London's Wembley Stadium, however, the Scots played with great heart. Don Hutchison scored for Scotland in the thirty-eighth minute. If the team scored just one more goal, the playoff would be tied. The Scots gave their all, and Christian Dailly looked liked he had scored a vital goal with a point-blank header. But England's goalkeeper, David Seaman, pulled off a tremendous save that preserved a slim advantage. The game ended 1–0. England had made it, but David realized that the team would have to play much better the next summer to stand a chance against the best teams in Europe.

David Beckham *(right)* poses with legendary English soccer star Bobby Charlton in the early 1990s.

David *(left)* and Gary Neville celebrate Manchester United's win of the Premiership Trophy during a celebration parade on May 12, 1996.

David played for Manchester United from 1994 to 2003.

David heads the ball away from his opponent during a 2003 Manchester United match.

David *(right)* was given a red card after fouling Argentinian captain Diego Simeone during England's second round match of the 1998 World Cup. His ejection led to a brutal reaction from fans and media, who blamed him for England's loss.

David puts the ball in play with a corner kick during a Real Madrid match against Dragon Team in Beijing, China. David played for Real Madrid from 2003 to 2007.

David's free kick scores the opening goal of England's match against Ecuador during the 2006 FIFA World Cup in Germany.

David married Victoria Adams, also known as Posh Spice, in 1999. They have three children, Brooklyn (shown here around age 3), Romeo, born in 2002, and Cruz, born in 2005.

David poses with kids from the David Beckham Academy in Los Angeles. David opened academies in Los Angeles and London to teach soccer to children of all ages and abilities.

David signs autographs for fans before a practice. He is one of the most recognized athletes in the world.

United fans will always remember the 1999–2000 season because the club did not participate in the FA Cup. The first World Club Championship was held in Brazil during January, when the FA Cup begins for Premiership teams. United was invited to take part because it won the previous season's Champions League. The tournament didn't go well for David or for United. David received a red card in the first match against Club Necaxa of Mexico, and United was eliminated in the next match, losing to Vasco da Gama of Brazil. Still, David thought the tournament was only a small failure because the time off gave him and his teammates a chance to recharge their batteries for the rest of the season.

The results seemed to back up David's claim. Despite the club's struggles to replace Peter Schmeichel (who had transferred to Sporting Lisbon of Portugal) in goal, it lost only three of thirty-eight matches and won the Premiership by eighteen points.

The ease with which United won the EPL and the club's absence from the FA Cup allowed the players to fully focus on the Champions League. The pivotal matches occurred in the quarterfinals. United was up against Real Madrid, the most successful club in the history of the Champions League. The first of two matches was held in Spain. It was an exciting contest, with plenty of chances for both teams, but somehow the game ended goalless. The draw meant that United needed to get a win back at Old Trafford, but Real settled matters with three goals in the first hour. David and Scholes got two late goals for United, which made the score look respectable. In David's view, the fact that they had pulled back two goals and their consistent form in the EPL spoke volumes about the club's character.

Real Madrid has won the European Cup/Champions League nine times. No other team has won it more than six times.

After the domestic season ended, the European Championship began. England was drawn into a tough group with Portugal, Germany, and Romania. England needed to finish first or second to move to the quarterfinals.

England started out superbly in the first match against Portugal in Eindhoven, Holland. The two countries have completely different styles of play. The Portuguese like to weave together long sequences of short passes to confuse a defense. The English, meanwhile, prefer to play the ball forward directly. For the first quarter of the match, England's style looked like it would win the day. Twice the ball was quickly played out wide to David on the right, and twice he arrowed in deadly crosses for Scholes and Steve McManaman to score. England's more direct style of play had helped it jump out to a 2–0 lead.

The Portuguese, however, didn't give up. They stuck to their patient passing game and produced two stunning goals. Luis Figo scored the first from well outside the penalty area with a blast into an upper corner. For the second, Portugal strung together two dozen or so passes before Rui Costa picked out Joao Pinto with a cross. England looked stunned. Matters only got worse after Michael Owen and McManaman were forced to leave because of injuries. Portugal took full advantage, and Nuno Gomes put them ahead to stay in the fifty-ninth minute. England had blown a two-goal lead for the first time since 1970. England's next opponent—Germany—was the team that had come from behind that year.

England's hopes looked dim. The loss to Portugal had been tough. England hadn't beaten the Germans in a tournament match since 1966. Even the English seemed to question whether they could get a positive result. Gary Lineker, one of England's greatest players, made a joke about the game of soccer. "Twenty-two men chase a ball for ninety minutes and in the end, the Germans win."

After the match in Eindhoven against Portugal, some of the English fans had taunted David and made horrible comments about his wife and child. Manager Kevin Keegan had witnessed what occurred and defended David publicly. "I'd have thumped them," Keegan said. "It was the worst thing I've seen in football. I've taken plenty of abuse in my time but this was way beyond anything I've heard. It was very personal." Much to David's delight, the whole country and the English fans attending the subsequent matches rallied around him. As he took the field against Germany for warm-ups, the England supporters began singing, "One David Beckham. There's only one David Beckham."

The moment sent shivers down David's spine. He said that it "meant the world" to him. "I really believe that events in Eindhoven finally helped people realize what I had been through after two years of abuse," he explained.

 David has several tattoos on his body. One of them is his wife's name, written in Hindi. He thought having her name written in English would be tacky.

The match itself was scrappy and physical. At first, neither team seemed able to mount an attack. David, though, was inspired. He created good opportunities for Owen and Scholes, and, just after halftime, England won a free kick just inside the German half, which David would take. The twenty-five-year-old midfielder angled a wicked ball into the German box to Alan Shearer, who beat the German keeper, Oliver Kahn, with a header. During the celebration, Gary Neville ran up to David and congratulated him. Shearer's goal decided the tense match, but Neville warned David not to get too carried away with celebrating. "We should get off the field. We haven't done anything yet," he said. "We haven't even qualified out of this group."

---

66 *You expect criticism from the media, and everyone has a right to their opinions. But it does affect the players more when it's from the fans than anyone else, because we set ourselves high standards and we want to do well for them. Fans pay a lot of money to watch us play. They expect a lot of us, and rightly so.* 99

—DAVID BECKHAM[44]

England still needed to get a draw against Romania to advance to the quarterfinals. England fell behind early, but Shearer and Owen each scored to put the team in front by halftime. The Romanians, though, were not through. They tied the match almost immediately after the restart and continued to press for the winner. Still, England looked like it would survive. However, in the eighty-ninth minute Phil Neville committed a penalty. Romania converted the resulting penalty kick, and England was out.

Phil Neville became the scapegoat, but the real fault, as Keegan pointed out, lay with the team's inability to pass consistently and to protect leads. "You have to ask if we can pass the ball better and control the game," Keegan said. "The answer in this tournament is that, sadly, we couldn't. You cannot spend sixty minutes chasing the ball, chasing the game, and expect to succeed at this level."

The team had fared poorly, but Keegan went out of his way to heap praise on David. "He has no ego. He is prepared to be a general if that is needed, and also a soldier if that is needed." David was no longer just a talented player. He was emerging as the team's leader.

Chapter | Eight

England Captain

Just a few months after the European Championship, England began its 2002 World Cup qualifying campaign. England's first game, in October 2000, was against the Germans—a team England had beaten four months earlier. It would be the last match ever played at old Wembley Stadium. To David, the game in that historic stadium seemed more like a party than a crucial qualifying match.

Unfortunately for England and its fans, the game itself didn't live up to the hype. Germany scored early on a free kick from Dietmar Hamann and simply kept England at bay for ninety minutes. England was outmanned in midfield and never really came close to scoring. David described the match as "awful, as frustrating as any I've ever played in." To make matters worse, he had to be taken out of the game after suffering a knee injury.

WEMBLEY STADIUM

Wembley Stadium opened in 1923. It was designed to hold 127,000 fans, but 200,000 came to watch that year's FA Cup final between Bolton Wanderers and West Ham United. Since then, the stadium has been the venue for most of England's international matches. The 1948 Olympic track-and-field competition and the 1966 World Cup final also took place there. The stadium was closed after the 2000 match against Germany so that it could be rebuilt. The new Wembley is scheduled to open in time to host the 2007 FA Cup.

Right after the match, Keegan resigned as England's manager. He told the players, "I have to be honest with you. And honest with myself. I've gone as far as I can with this. I'm calling it a day. You've got good times ahead of you. You're very good players."

England had to continue the qualifying round without him or any long-term replacement. Instead, two temporary managers took over. The second of those, Peter Taylor, named David as his captain. David had never openly asked for the job, but he considered it an honor. Taylor called, at eight in the morning, to break the good news.

"Sorry to ring this early but I'm about to announce the squad," he told David. "I've picked a young group and some new young players. I think the right thing is for you to captain them. I've got absolutely no doubt about you being ready for the job." Many critics felt that David was not vocal enough to lead his teammates, but he felt confident that he could lead by working hard and setting a good example.

At Manchester United, however, Roy Keane was still the captain. Unlike David, Keane preferred to lead by yelling first and asking questions later. His methods might have rubbed some of his teammates the wrong way, but they couldn't argue with the results.

In 2001 United captured its seventh Premiership title in nine years and the sixth in the seven years that David had been a starter. Such are the standards at the club, however, that club leaders began talking about major changes after the team was eliminated by Bayern Munich in the quarterfinals of the Champions League. Keane was the most outspoken. "We're just not good enough. We're average. Maybe it's time to move on, maybe it's the end of the road for this team."

David was not one of Keane's targets. He was arguably in the best form of his life. England had finally named a permanent manager, Sven-Goran Eriksson. The new boss informed David that he would remain captain. "I think you'll make a great

England captain," Eriksson told him. "You're a good enough player and a player others can look up to. Anybody who doubts that, it's your job to prove them wrong."

 Swedish-born Sven-Goran Eriksson was the first foreigner ever hired to manage the English national team. His tenure ended after the 2006 World Cup.

David came to feel equally confident in the new boss. Eriksson was a calm presence on the team, and the players respected and listened to him. Their faith in one another was justified by the results England earned on the field. David scored three goals as Eriksson became the first England manager to win his first five matches in charge. Many had written off England's chances of winning its qualifying group after the disaster against Germany. But with the hot streak, the team controlled its own fate. There was just the small matter of beating the Germans in Munich, Germany.

The Germans were heavily favored. David realized the size of England's task and wondered whether anyone could ever beat Germany on their own field. David's groin was slightly strained, which meant he couldn't train with his teammates until the day before the match. But the confidence Eriksson showed made everyone, including David, like their chances.

Before the match, Eriksson told his players to enjoy themselves. He told them that they were better than the Germans and that they could beat them if they believed in themselves. The players may have been inspired, but before they knew what hit them, they were a goal behind. David and his teammates kept their composure. Michael Owen tied the score at one, and Steven Gerrard put England ahead right before the half with an explosive shot from just outside the penalty area.

Scoring right before the half usually gives a team a big boost, but David felt more nervous than he had before the match. He wasn't sure whether England should try to protect the lead by playing defensively or try to get another goal to wrap up the match. Eriksson told the players that they had struck the right balance between offense and defense in the first half. If they did that in the second half, they would likely score more goals.

He was right. Owen scored right after the match restarted, and then he scored again. Scholes set up Emile Heskey for a fifth goal. There were still twenty minutes left—or, as David put it, "twenty minutes in soccer heaven." England would have liked to beat the Germans 10–1, but they had to be satisfied with keeping possession and frustrating their old rival. The players, the fans, and the nation rejoiced. This was England's best soccer achievement since it won the 1966 World Cup. The players had every right to feel proud.

 In 1966 England beat West Germany 4–2 at Wembley to claim its only World Cup.

After the match, Gary Neville reminded his teammates that they still had to win against Albania and Greece to clinch the group. Their performance against Albania was labored, but they still won 2–0. The game against Greece in October, however, proved to be more difficult.

Perhaps the month between matches had given the team too much time to think about what was at stake. The players were nervous before the match. The locker room was unusually quiet. Eriksson broke the silence by advising his team to pass the ball to one another quickly. The advice was sound, but England struggled to follow it on the field.

The Greeks had no chance of qualifying, but they were pumped up for the match. They ran hard and challenged every ball, even many of the ones that weren't loose. England couldn't establish any rhythm and didn't seem able to mount a scoring threat. And then disaster really struck. The Greeks got a sloppy goal right before the half. David found himself wondering whether England could at least get a draw.

During halftime, Eriksson told his team that they were letting the Greeks control the match. He encouraged his players to raise the tempo and take the game to their opponents. David took his advice to heart and played a captain's part. He seemed to be playing all four midfield positions at the same time. He was winning balls, making his trademark passes, and even beating opponents off the dribble, which is not something he normally does.

The inspiration came from within. David was angry. He was mad that the Greeks were having their way with England. He was hot and tired, and he wanted to do something about it. He was determined to make a difference.

 David likes to spend his money on expensive vehicles. His cars include a Hummer, a Ferrari, and a Lamborghini.

David's efforts were rewarded when he drew a free kick. However, this was the one part of his game that was weak. His free kicks kept going high or wide or both high and wide at the same time. As he lined up, Teddy Sheringham told him, "Watch me. Just watch me." David took his advice and repeated a routine that they had practiced at United many times. He played the ball into an open space near Greece's goal, and Sheringham headed the ball over the goalkeeper into the far corner. The score was tied at one.

England needed just one more goal to win. Or at least that was all they needed until Greece went right down the field and scored again. David wondered if it was all over right then.

England kept on working hard and winning free kicks, but David kept squandering them. With only seconds remaining, Sheringham won one last free kick ten yards outside the Greek penalty area. He wanted to take the free kick himself, but as the team captain, David decided that it was too far away from the goal for Sheringham. David took a couple of breaths and tried to gather himself. He bent the ball over the Greek wall, and it swerved into the upper left-hand corner of the net.

David had just beaten the Greek goalkeeper from more than twenty-five yards away. He ran with his arms outstretched toward the fans before his teammates mobbed him. Martin Keown, who has a reputation for being a serious defender, ran up to him laughing and screamed, "That's amazing. That's amazing. That's why you're the man."

The match was still tied. A draw would mean that if Germany beat Finland—a game that was happening at the same time—the Germans would qualify instead of England. But David had learned that Germany's match was tied and nearly over. England won a throw-in after a failed Greek attack. The ball came to David, who just booted the ball as high as he could as the final whistle blew.

 Greece's good performance in the World Cup qualifying round was no fluke. In 2004 the Greeks shocked the soccer world by winning the European Championship.

The players were celebrating, but everyone went silent when the PA announcer interrupted to give the final score of Germany's match: Germany 0, Finland 0. England—in large part thanks to Finland—was on its way to the World Cup.

Chapter Nine

The End of an Era

The months leading to the 2002 World Cup did not go well for David. Manchester United failed to win the Premiership, or win any trophy for that matter, for the first time since 1998. Arsenal clinched the title at Old Trafford—a humiliating defeat for United. The team also trailed Liverpool. For the first time since 1991, the club had fallen below second place. In the FA Cup, Middlesbrough eliminated United in the fourth round. The players' hopes of salvaging the season by winning the Champions League were dashed when German club Bayer Leverkusen got the better of them in the semifinals.

Ferguson blew his top with the media after the Arsenal match. He angrily rejected suggestions that Keane didn't have a suitable partner in midfield and that the central defenders were simply not good enough. In David's view, the departure of assistant coach Steve McClaren, who ran the practices, had unsettled the team. He was a great communicator who knew how to teach players and make the lessons enjoyable.

 Steve McClaren was appointed coach of England's national team after the 2006 World Cup.

During this same period, David's life went through a series of ups and downs. His parents filed for a divorce after being married for thirty-two years. A couple of months later, he learned that Victoria was pregnant with their second child. National coaches worldwide voted him second, behind Luis Figo, for the World Player of the Year award. He also signed a new lucrative contract with Manchester United. But his chances of playing in the World Cup were in question after he broke his left foot during a Champions League quarterfinal match against the Spanish team Deportivo de La Coruna.

Initially, doctors feared that David would be out as long as eight weeks. If that was the case, he wouldn't have enough time to be in shape for the World Cup. David went through intensive rehabilitation, lasting several hours every day. His foot recovered by early May, when England began its journey to Japan and South Korea for the World Cup. But that didn't guarantee he would be ready to play. He still had to regain his sharpness and match fitness first. David built his stamina by running in a swimming pool. He strengthened his injured foot by learning to balance on a trampoline. And he sharpened his reflexes by trapping and volleying balls that were thrown at him.

Japan and South Korea cohosted the 2002 World Cup. It is the only time that two countries have been chosen to stage the tournament.

All the hard work paid off. David was ready for the first match against Sweden. He was justifiably excited, but the match didn't quite live up to expectations. He did set up England's first goal with a corner kick that Sol Campbell headed home. But England never really found its groove, and the Swedes came back to earn a draw. Even though it wasn't a great result, a draw was good enough, especially after the dramatic win over Argentina that followed. England also had a 0–0 draw against Nigeria in its last group match. England was on top of the group and had to play Denmark for the right to advance.

David was worried about the match because Denmark, like Sweden, was well organized and physical. Furthermore, the

Danes knew England well because many of the Danish players played in the Premiership. And finally, he feared that his teammates would be looking ahead to a possible quarterfinal clash with powerful Brazil. He realized that he was mistaken as soon as he walked into the locker room. His teammates looked focused and confident, like they had before the Argentina match. The Danes, meanwhile, looked nervous the minute they took the field.

Five minutes into the game, David set up the first goal with a corner kick. Owen scored fifteen minutes later, and Emile Heskey put the match in England's pocket just before halftime. The only downside was that David's foot felt bad for the first time since rehab had ended. He attributed it to the fact that he had to wear shoes with long studs (cleats) because it was raining in Nigata, Japan. Before the match, most of his discomfort had been on top of the foot. But afterward, the bottom of his foot hurt. He felt like the studs on his shoes were pressing into the injury with every step he took.

David didn't have to worry about rain in the quarterfinals, though. In fact, it was the heat in Shizuoka, Japan, that worried David. Most people felt that rain favored the English and that hot weather favored the Brazilians because of the different climates in the two countries. Even David later admitted that his heart sank when he woke up and discovered that the sun was shining brightly.

Bend It Like Beckham

In 2002 a British film titled *Bend It Like Beckham* honored David's ability to make the ball turn, or bend, in the air. The movie, about two young girls in England who join a soccer team, got great reviews. Although it wasn't really about David, the title helped increase his name recognition around the world, especially in the United States. Victoria even contributed a song to the film's sound track.

England started out conservatively. The Brazilians liked to attack, so Eriksson told his players to keep defensive shape and attack after the Brazilians overcommitted. The plan worked perfectly midway through the first half. Emile Heskey made a thirty-yard pass to Michael Owen. One of Brazil's defenders should have intercepted it. But he wasn't paying attention and the ball bounced to Owen, who reacted quickly to beat the Brazilian goalkeeper.

David felt elated at the prospect of beating the most famous soccer team in the world. "I was forty yards away," he said of the goal. "It was like watching it on television. Michael Owen scoring for England against Brazil. I don't believe this is happening."

Most opponents would have been let down and anxious. But a few minutes before the end of the first half, David noticed that the great Brazilian striker Ronaldo and the referee were sharing a joke. He couldn't believe it. It just showed him the confidence of the Brazilian players. David knew that the match was far from over.

A few minutes later—moments before the half—a loose ball was rolling toward David. He jumped over it in the hope that it would go out of bounds. Somehow Roberto Carlos kept the ball in play, and the Brazilians moved into England's penalty area in a matter of seconds. Ronaldinho then quickly set up Rivaldo for a strike that beat David Seaman. David felt terrible. Suddenly Brazil had taken away England's momentum.

Eriksson sensed the mood and tried to refocus the players. "We played well," he told them. "We should be winning 1–0. We've got to tidy things up, make sure we don't give away silly goals, and then we'll get our chances."

Five minutes after the half, England gave up what may or may not have been a silly goal. Brazil had a free kick about forty yards away from England's goal, which normally means that the player taking the kick will cross the ball rather than shoot. Ronaldinho, however, noticed that David Seaman liked to leave his goal a split second before the ball was kicked so that he could cover more crosses. Ronaldinho caught him and lofted the ball over his head and into the English net. Many, including David, believed that Ronaldinho miskicked a pass, but the Brazilian insisted that he had intended to shoot the ball. In either case, Brazil was up 2–1.

Ronaldinho got red-carded five minutes later, but it didn't help England. The 100-degree temperature and the two goals in the space of five minutes had sapped all their energy and will. Brazil went on to win the World Cup, but David felt devastated because he thought that England had given away the game.

Brazil has been the most successful nation in World Cup history. The nation has won the tournament five times, in 1958, 1962, 1970, 1994, and 2002.

The Beckhams' second child, Romeo, was born on September 1, 2002, less than a month after the 2002–2003 season began. Manchester United started the season like the last one had never ended. The team fell behind Arsenal in the Premiership. Arsenal also eliminated United at Old Trafford in the fifth round of the FA Cup. Arsenal won 2–0, and the second goal, which involved an intricate series of passes, seemed to underline its superiority.

After the match, a furious Ferguson blamed David for the second goal. Ferguson later admitted that a number of players had made mistakes, but that day's argument with David had huge repercussions. David defended himself, angering the boss so much that he accidentally kicked a shoe into the star mid-fielder's face. The resulting cut above David's right eye required stitches and badly damaged their relationship.

As a celebrity couple, David and Victoria face some extra risks to their personal safety. In 2002 police arrested nine people on charges that they planned to kidnap Victoria and hold her for ransom. The criminals might have also been planning to take David and Victoria's children.

United went on an amazing run after that match. The club won fifteen of its last eighteen Premiership matches to overtake Arsenal and win the title. But David didn't feel as good as he had been after the previous championships. He played every minute of the last three matches of the season, but Ferguson had benched him for some crucial matches, including a 2–2 draw against Arsenal in London. The message was clear. David realized that his time with the only club he had ever wanted to play for was nearing its end.

Chapter Ten

Beckham's Reign in Spain

Rumors that twenty-seven-year-old David Beckham would be transferring to Real Madrid, the most successful club in the history of soccer, surfaced in the early months of 2003. Real president Florentino Pérez denied that there was any truth to the stories. "Never, never, never, seven times never" was his response when first asked. But few believed him, especially after Manchester United played Real in the quarterfinals of the 2003 Champions League.

Real Madrid paid very little attention to defense. Most of the club's players were permitted to attack whenever they saw an opportunity. They dared opponents to do the same. Manchester United tried to exploit the gaps in Real's defense in the first half, but they didn't score. Real Madrid took advantage. Twelve minutes into the game, Luis Figo exchanged passes with Zinedine Zidane and found himself on the left wing. Most players would have crossed the ball, but he lofted the ball over Manchester United goalkeeper Fabien Barthez's head. It bounced off of the far post and into the net.

In the twenty-eighth minute, Zidane made a pass to Raul in the penalty box. The Spanish striker spun and shot low inside the near post. The stunning quality of both goals and the attacking freedom Real Madrid's players enjoyed left David in awe. "When they had the ball, they were making runs all over the place," he later wrote. "It might have looked like we were standing back, watching them play. I think the truth was they were getting so many players involved every time they came forward that we found ourselves defending one man against three all over the field."

The final score was 3–1, which meant the odds were stacked against United advancing to the semifinals. Still, David was excited about playing the second match against Real Madrid at Old Trafford. The game offered him another chance to match wits and skills with the most creative club in the world. He was understandably devastated when Ferguson started Juan Veron, who had been out injured for months, instead.

Veron played well and United scored twice, but Ronaldo scored three times for Real Madrid. Ferguson substituted David for Veron in the second half, and the tone of the match changed completely. David angled the ball into the upper right-hand corner of

Real's net with a free kick and outhustled a Spanish defender to score again. Only five minutes remained. United could have advanced by scoring twice more, but a free kick off David's foot went high and Ole Gunnar Solskjaer could not quite latch on to one of his famous crosses.

United was out of the Champions League, but David had been brilliant. In the locker room, Ferguson told him, "You played well, David." Several Real players asked to exchange jerseys with him, and Roberto Carlos, one of Real's stars, asked, "Are you coming to play for us?"

David had never considered playing for another club, but the way Ferguson was pushing him to the sidelines made him realize that he was ready to leave. Ferguson thought David's lavish lifestyle off the field was harming his play on it. "He was blessed with great stamina, the best of all players I've had here," Ferguson said. "After training, he'd always be practicing, practicing, practicing. But his life changed when he met his wife. She's in pop and David got another image. He developed this 'fashion thing.' I saw his transition to a different person." For his part, David has said that his endorsement career (promoting products such as Coca-Cola and IBM), his modeling career (his good looks have earned him cover appearances on magazines such as *Vanity Fair*), his celebrity wife, and his taste for the finer things in life have never come between him and soccer.

In June, David and his family were vacationing in California when Manchester United released a statement informing the fans and press—and David—that the club had agreed to sell him to Barcelona. David felt betrayed because United had not told him first. More important, he didn't want to go to Barcelona. Immediately, he and his advisers arranged for him to be transferred to Real Madrid instead. David was sad to leave the club he had been with for his whole professional life, especially since it was his dad's favorite club. But he was also excited to be going to the most successful club in the world.

David expressed his excitement during his first press conference in Madrid. "I have always loved soccer," he told reporters. "Of course I love my family and I have a wonderful life. But soccer is everything to me. To play for Real is a dream come true. Thank you to everyone for being here to share my arrival. *Gracias* (Thank you)."

David knew that playing in Spain would be a big change. He took some Spanish lessons, but he also knew that many of his teammates spoke English and other languages. In addition team translators would always be around to help. One way or another, he'd get by.

Even before he arrived, the Spanish public knew that David had style. But they were stunned to find out how much substance his game had during a preseason tour of East Asia. In contrast to what Ferguson had claimed, they were especially impressed by his hard work and commitment. After his first match, one Spanish paper complimented his "sense of responsibility" and observed that "he never showed off."

"Real Madrid is a great club. It was the one I wanted, the only team I could see myself playing [for]. There are so many world-class players [on] this squad. Also, you can see from the atmosphere and in the way the players get on with one another that there is a great team spirit, which I like."

—DAVID BECKHAM ON HIS NEW TEAM

Real Madrid started the 2003–2004 season well. Before 2003 ended, the team had advanced to the second round of the Champions League and moved into first place in the Spanish League. The key match came in early December against Barcelona. Real had not won a league match at Barcelona in twenty years. In the thirty-seventh minute, David split the Barcelona defense with a pinpoint pass to Zidane. Zidane laid the ball back to Roberto Carlos in front of the Barcelona penalty box. Carlos shot the ball so hard that it rebounded off goal-keeper Victor Valdez and into the net. David fought for every ball and created more chances for others. He didn't set up any more goals, but his teammates attributed the 2–1 victory to his "never-say-die English attitude."

The players' hope of winning three major trophies died in March and April 2004. First they lost the Spanish Cup final 3–2 to Zaragoza. Then Monaco eliminated them from the Champions League in the quarterfinals. Finally they lost an eight-point lead and finished third behind Valencia and Barcelona in the Spanish League. Most experts agree that the club's failures weren't David's fault. The problem was that the team spent too little time defending. The club had many star players, so fewer men were on the field to play the important supporting roles.

After his first season in Madrid, David captained England in the 2004 European Championship, which was held in Portugal. The team's first match was against France. England played well and took the lead a few minutes before the half, when David's free kick set up Frank Lampard for a header from the right side-line. In the second half, Wayne Rooney, England's eighteen-year-old prodigy, ran through the French defense and drew a penalty. David took the penalty kick. He struck the ball well, but French goalkeeper Fabien Barthez guessed that shot would go to his right and flung himself toward the post to make the save. England still looked like it was going to win the match, but

Zinedine Zidane, David's teammate at Real, scored with a free kick late in the match. Then matters got worse. Thierry Henry drew a penalty for France, and Zidane converted to give the French a 2–1 win.

The loss was shocking, but England's players knew they could still advance to the quarterfinals if they could beat Switzerland and Croatia. They struggled during the first twenty minutes of the Switzerland match, but Gerrard, David, and Owen set up Rooney for a header to put England ahead. Rooney scored again in the seventy-fifth minute with a hard shot, and Gerrard rounded off a fine match with a goal in the eighty-second minute.

The 3–0 win meant that England needed only a draw against Croatia to advance. Rooney's power and skill were too much for Croatia. England fell behind 1–0, but Rooney set up Scholes and thumped in a shot of his own from twenty-five yards out before the half. In the second half, he exchanged passes with Owen before scoring his second. Lampard also scored to make the final score 4–2.

England's opponent in the quarterfinal was the host nation, Portugal. Playing the host is never an easy task, but England jumped to a lead in the third minute after Owen flicked the ball past Portugal's last defender and then raced in to score. The momentum changed in the twenty-seventh minute, when Rooney left the match with a foot injury. England didn't have enough size up front, and Portugal began to bear down on them. The pressure paid off with just seven minutes left. Helder Postiga scored from just outside the penalty box.

The match went to extra time. Portugal was flowing and scored when Rui Costa finished off a breathtaking move that went from one end of the field to the other. The English looked like they were through, but David set up the tying goal for Lampard from a corner with just five minutes left. When no one else scored, the match had to be settled by penalty kicks. England had been eliminated from the 1990 and 1998 World Cups, as well as from the 1996 European Championship, by penalty kicks. The team's bad luck continued. David completely scuffed his attempt, and Darius Vassell's shot was saved by the Portuguese keeper Ricardo. Eriksson expressed the dejection everyone felt. "To get over this will take more than twenty-four hours, much longer."

 Before the penalty-kick tiebreaker came into effect in 1976, matches that were tied after 120 minutes were settled with a replay match or by flipping a coin.

The bad news just kept coming for David. Real Madrid's 2004–2005 season was even worse than 2003–2004. The team finished second, just four points behind Barcelona in the Spanish League, but Barcelona had been in control throughout the season. Real was also eliminated before the quarterfinals by Valladolid in the Spanish Cup and by Juventus in the Champions League. This outcome wouldn't be a bad season for most clubs, but it was disaster for Real Madrid. Two coaches were fired during the season, and fans began to call for the club's president to resign. David didn't face all bad news, though. In February 2005, Victoria gave birth to the couple's third son, Cruz David Beckham.

Real's 2005–2006 season didn't improve much. The club finished twelve points behind Barcelona in the league. Arsenal eliminated Real from the Champions League in the round of sixteen. The players' only hope for a major trophy was the Spanish Cup. They advanced to the semifinals, where they met Zaragoza. Their chances of salvaging the season looked bleak after they lost the first match in Zaragoza 6–1.

 In Spain, club presidents are elected by dues-paying club members, called *socios*. A club like Barcelona or Real Madrid has more than 100,000 socios.

The second match started out much better. Just two minutes into it, David took a corner kick from the left. The defense cleared the ball, but it bounced outside the penalty area to Cicinho, who fired a hard shot into the upper-left corner of the net. Three minutes later, David crossed the ball from the right to Ronaldo in the penalty area. He quickly laid the ball off to Robinho. Robinho skimmed it across the ground and into the back of the net. Five minutes after that, David lofted a pass into the penalty area from forty yards away on the right sideline. Ronaldo streaked in and stabbed the ball past the goalkeeper with his left foot. The score was 3–0 after only ten minutes. Real needed to score just two more goals to advance to the final.

Real continued to attack but didn't score again in the first half. In the sixteenth minute of the second half, David won a free kick thirty yards to the right of Zaragoza's goal. He gently rolled the ball to Zidane, who left it for Carlos. Carlos, who may have the hardest shot in soccer, rocketed the ball into the upper left-hand corner of the net. Real needed one more goal. The team threw almost every player forward, but the vital goal just would not come. Real won 4–0 but lost 6–5 on total score. The loss meant that Real had failed to win a major trophy for the third straight season. That hadn't happened since 1953. Still, the fans gave the club a standing ovation as they left the field. They knew that the players had given everything they had.

Next David shifted his attention back to the international game for the 2006 World Cup. England started out brilliantly in its first match against Paraguay. Paraguay's captain, Carlos Gamarra, accidentally headed one of David's free kicks into his own net. This early goal should have given the English confidence and forced Paraguay to try to attack, but neither occurred. The English couldn't string together their passes, and Paraguay was too afraid of them to take any risks. England won the match, but it wasn't pretty. The players needed to play much better if they hoped to win the World Cup.

With a population of almost 1.1 million, Trinidad and Tobago was the smallest nation to qualify for the 2006 World Cup.

England had a similar lack of fluidity in the next match, against Trinidad and Tobago. England didn't pass the ball well until Wayne Rooney and Aaron Lennon entered the game in the fifty-eighth minute. David normally plays on the right wing, but he dropped back to right fullback so that Lennon could take his position. In the eighty-second minute, David launched a free kick into the penalty area to Peter Crouch, England's tall forward.

Crouch rose above the defender and headed the ball into the net. During injury time, Gerrard eluded a defender and fired an unstoppable shot from just outside the top of the penalty box. The 2–0 final score looked good, but England's players knew that they had struggled against a weaker team.

The team played much better in the first half of the final first-round match, against Sweden. After a series of promising attacks, Joe Cole hit a dipping shot into the right-hand corner of the Sweden's net. But England's defense looked confused in the second half. The team struggled to cope with cross passes and couldn't clear the ball out of its own half of the field. In the fifty-first minute, Sweden's Tobias Linderoth whipped the ball into the area from the left to Marcus Allback. Alback used his head to flick the ball past keeper Paul Robinson into the far corner. The Swedes hit the bar twice more after corner kicks. England scored next after Gerrard headed home a chipped pass from Cole. It appeared that England was going to steal the match, but the defense gave Sweden a second goal. They failed to clear a throw-in from the left, and Sweden's Henrik Larsson managed to redirect the ball past Robinson.

Despite the loss, England had qualified for the round of sixteen, where it faced Ecuador. The players struggled to connect their passes again, but Ecuador's players weren't performing any better. The game dragged on until the sixtieth minute.

England won a free kick just outside of Ecuador's penalty area. David lifted the ball over the wall and down into the right-hand corner of the net. Neither team came close to scoring the rest of the match. England was still playing poorly, but it had reached the quarterfinals of the World Cup.

England's opponent was Portugal. This match wasn't nearly as well played as the one between the two teams two years earlier. Both teams were cautious, and neither came close to scoring. Rooney received a red card for stomping on a Portuguese player in the second half. But even playing eleven men on ten didn't inspire the Portuguese. The match went to penalty kicks, and England lost again. David played a part in nearly every positive thing that England did. But the team just never came together, and it simply couldn't win a penalty shootout. Eriksson could only shake his head after the match. "We practiced penalties so much I really don't know what more we could do about it." Once again, England went home in disappointment. Italy beat France 5–3 to win the 2006 World Cup Final.

A Bright Future

President Florentino Pérez had built Real Madrid around David and a group of superstars (whom the Spanish refer to as Galacticos), but he neglected to sign a good supporting cast and defenders. Since the club failed to win any major trophies for three years, Pérez was forced to resign as president before the 2005–2006 season ended. The club elected a new president, Ramón Calderón.

Shortly after the 2006 World Cup, David resigned as England's team captain. He still hopes to be part of the national squad, though. New manager Steve McClaren, who coached David at Manchester United, hasn't closed the door to including David on the team in the future. However, McClaren didn't include David in the squad that began England's qualification campaign for the 2008 European Championship. (Qualifying matches begin a year before the tournament.)

Entering the 2006–2007 season, David was still clearly part of the Real's plans. In August 2006, he and the club announced that negotiations to extend his contract had begun. David told Calderón that he and his family were happy in Madrid. And Calderón expressed how satisfied he was with David's performances on the field and what he represents as a person. But injuries and disagreements with his coach, Fabio Capello, kept David out of most of the action through the early part of the 2006–2007 season. Most famously, David clashed with Capello about his desire to attend the wedding of friends Tom Cruise and Katie Holmes. Even though David was injured, Capello wanted him on the sidelines for the team's game that day.

By early 2007, David was ready for a change. He had long expressed a desire to play soccer in the United States. He had already set up his soccer training camp, the David Beckham Academy, outside Los Angeles, California. A life in Los Angeles would help David and Victoria pursue careers in the entertainment industry. So, few people were surprised when in January 2007, David announced that he would be leaving Real Madrid at the end of the 2006–2007 season to join the Los Angeles Galaxy of Major League Soccer (MLS).

What was surprising was the contract that he signed. It called for a reported $250 million over five years. At an average of $50 million per year, the thirty-one-year-old became the highest-paid athlete in the history of team sports. Even more shocking was that such a salary could come to a player in the MLS, a league that doesn't draw big crowds and television contracts.

While David was thrilled with the money, he said that wasn't his reason for joining the Galaxy and MLS. "This move for me is not about the money," he said. "It's about hopefully making a difference in the [United States] with the soccer and that's what I'm going there for. I'm going for the life, of course, for my kids to enjoy it and my wife to enjoy it, but the main thing for me is to improve the soccer and to improve the standard and to be part of history really."

David's signing was the talk of the sports world. MLS, which has trouble gaining any headlines in the United States, was front-page news. People who knew next to nothing about soccer were talking about David.

In March David was in the news again after he sprained his right knee. Doctors said he wouldn't play for at least one month. The injury wasn't expected to affect his start with the Galaxy.

Only time will tell whether David will be able to carry the Galaxy to the top of the league and to bring soccer to the forefront of the U.S. sports scene. But David Beckham is undoubtedly the most famous name in soccer, and his star power can only help the league.

PERSONAL STATISTICS

Name:

David Robert Joseph Beckham

Nickname:

Becks

Position:

Midfielder

Born:

May 2, 1975

Birthplace:

Leytonstone, London, England

Height:

6' 0"

Weight:

165 pounds

CAREER CLUB STATISTICS

		League Play		European Play	
Season	Team	Games	Goals	Games	Goals
1994–95	Preston	5	2	0	0
1994–95	M. United	4	0	1	1
1995–96	M. United	33	7	2	0
1996–97	M. United	36	7	10	2
1997–98	M. United	37	9	8	0
1998–99	M. United	34	6	12	2
1999–00	M. United	31	6	12	2
2000–01	M. United	31	9	12	0
2001–02	M. United	28	11	13	5
2002–03	M. United	31	6	13	3
2003–04	R. Madrid	32	3	7	1
2004–05	R. Madrid	30	4	8	0
2005–06	R. Madrid	31	3	7	1

GLOSSARY

Champions League: a yearly tournament that brings together the top soccer clubs in Europe (not national teams)

corner kick: a chance to kick that is awarded when the defending team plays the ball out of bounds behind its own goal line. A member of the offensive team takes a free kick from the corner closest to where the ball went out of bounds.

cross: a pass that goes laterally across the field

English Premier League (EPL): the most prestigious competitive soccer grouping in England. The EPL champion is the EPL team that has the most points at the end of the soccer season. The EPL is also known as the Premiership. It used to be called the First Division.

European Football Championship: also called the European Championship, this tournament is for European national soccer teams. It takes place every four years.

extra time: a thirty-minute overtime session added to tie games at the end of regulation

FA Cup: also known as the Football Association Challenge Cup, this tournament involves clubs from all levels of the

English football (soccer) league system. The FA Final takes place at the end of the soccer season in May.

free kick: a chance to kick that is awarded by the referee for fouls outside the penalty area. Free kicks are taken from the spot where the foul took place.

injury time: time added to the end of regulation to make up for stoppages due to injuries

midfielder: a soccer player who both attacks and defends

penalty kick: a chance to kick that is awarded to a player after certain penalties. In tournament play, penalty kicks also decide a match that remains tied after extra time.

red card: a punishment for excessive roughness. A red-carded player must leave the match, and the team is not allowed to substitute another player.

tackle: a move in which one soccer player uses his legs to break up the dribble of an opponent

wall: a group of defenders standing close together in front of the goal on a penalty kick

World Cup: the international soccer competition that takes place every four years. The Cup brings together thirty-two national teams for a month-long tournament.

SOURCES

3   David Beckham, *Beckham: Both Feet on the Ground* (New York: HarperCollins, 2004), 263.

4   Ibid.

8   bid., 9.

11   Jimmy Burns, *When Beckham Went to Spain: Power, Stardom and Real Madrid* (London: Penguin, 2004), 94.

11–12   Victoria Blackburn, *David Beckham: The Great Betrayal* (London: John Blake Publishing, 2003), 27.

12   Burns, *When Beckham Went to Spain*, 93.

13–14   Beckham, *Beckham*, 23.

14   Ibid.

15   Ibid., 24.

16   Ibid., 29.

17   Blackburn, *David Beckham*, 32.

17   Ibid, 34.

18   Ibid., 32.

20   Ibid., 40.

20–21   Ibid., 40.

22   Beckham, *Beckham*, 43.

25   Blackburn, *David Beckham*, 42.

26   Beckham, *Beckham*, 56.

27   Blackburn, *David Beckham*, 43.

31–32   Burns, *When Beckham Went to Spain*, 99.

32   Blackburn, *David Beckham*, 43.

34   Beckham, *Beckham*, 65.

36   Ibid., 76.

37   Ibid., 9.

38   Blackburn, *David Beckham*, 45.

39   Beckham, *Beckham*, 82.

40   Ibid., 109.

40   Burns, *When Beckham Went to Spain*,103.

43   Blackburn, *David Beckham*, 52.

43–44   Burns, *When Beckham Went to Spain*, 104.

46   Blackburn, *David Beckham*, 96.

46   Beckham, *Beckham*, 131.

47   Ibid.,136.

49   Burns, *When Beckham Went to Spain*, 114.

51   Beckham, *Beckham*, 150.

51   Ibid., 151.

61   John F. Molinaro. "Brazil Always Wins in the End." *CBC.ca* http://www.cbc.ca/sports/worldcup2006/

features/brazil.html (November 9, 2006).

62   Blackburn, *David Beckham*, 182.

62   Beckham, *Beckham*, 196.

63   Ibid.

63   Justyn Barnes, "Most Wanted," *Manchester United Magazine*, 37.

64   *World Soccer*, July 2000, 21.

64   Beckham, *Beckham*, 117.

65   Ibid., 199.

66   Ibid., 200.

67   Ibid., 203.

67   Gavin Hamilton, "Record Ruud Signals United Intent," *World Soccer*, June 2001, 58.

67–68   Beckham, *Beckham*, 206.

69   Ibid., 214.

72   Ibid., 229.

72   Ibid., 231.

78   Ibid., 273.

79   Ibid., 275.

82   Sid Lowe, "The Circus Starts Here," *World Soccer*, August 2003, 5.

83   Beckham, *Beckham*, 330.

84   Ibid., 340.

84   Ibid., 39.

84   Blackburn, *David Beckham*, 22.

85   Beckham, *Beckham*, 366.

86   Sid Lowe, "Becks Appeal," *World Soccer*, September 2003, 15.

86   *League Magazine*, "A Word with . . . Beckham," October 2004, 17.

87   Sid Lowe, "Tango at the Top," *World Soccer*, February 2004, 18.

89   Gavin Hamilton, "Ricardo Outshines Big Time Charlies," *World Soccer*, August 2004, 55.

94   John Haydon, "Portugal Slips Past England," *WashingtonTimes.com*, July 2, 2006, http://www.washingtontimes.com/sports/20060702-123921-8368r.htm (Feburary 16, 2006).)

97   "Beckham Admits Pay Packet is an 'Amazing Sum,'" *Soccernet.espn.go.com*, n.d., http://soccernet.espn.go.com/news/story?id=399613&cc=5901 (January 12, 2007).

BIBLIOGRAPHY

Beckham, David. *Beckham: Both Feet on the Ground.* New York: HarperCollins, 2003.

Blackburn, Victoria. *David Beckham: The Great Betrayal.* London: John Blake Publishing, 2003.

Burns, Jimmy. *When Beckham Went to Spain: Power, Stardom and Real Madrid.* London: Penguin, 2004.

Carlin, John. *White Angels: Beckham, Real Madrid, and the New Football.* New York: Bloomsbury, 2004.

Gifford, Clive. *So You Think You Know David Beckham?* London: Hodder Children's Books, 2003.

WEBSITES

Beckham Mania

http://www.beckhammania.com/

This site follows all of the latest David Beckham news, with a bio, photos, links, and more.

The David Beckham Academy

http://www.thedavidbeckhamacademy.com/main.html

The official site of David's soccer academy includes schedules, registration information, and a photo gallery.

MLSnet

http://web.mlsnet.com

The home page of Major League Soccer includes all of the latest news on the league, with scores, video highlights, and statistics.

Soccernet ESPN

http://soccernet.espn.go.com

ESPN's page is devoted to soccer clubs from around the world as well as international competition. Enjoy scores, schedules, stats, news updates, and more.

INDEX